thanks a bunch

We're here to brighten each other's days.
To show small kindnesses. To change things
for the better. And when someone with a generous
spirit comes into our lives, even the little things
they do make a lasting difference.

You are one of those people.
You give of yourself. You make the world
more beautiful. Thank you for everything you do.
Thank you for the person you are.

Let us be grateful to people who make us happy; they are the charming gardeners who make our souls blossom.

MARCEL PROUST

You have a way of
brightening the day.
every Monday!

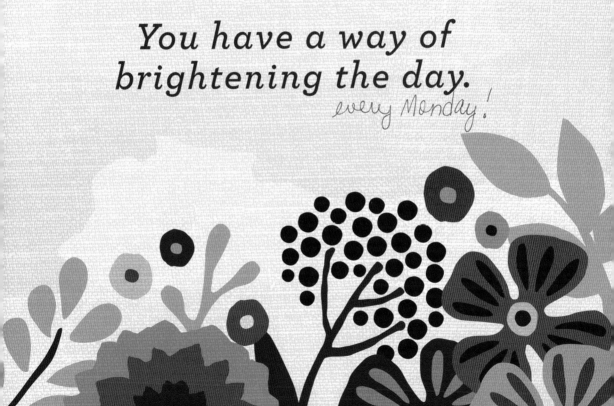

○

...whatever good we give
out completes the circle
and comes back to us.

FLORA EDWARDS

Set good things in motion.

Act as if what you do makes
a difference. It does.

WILLIAM JAMES

Trust in your power to change things for the better.

I thank you for your kindness,
I will not soon forget...

JOANNA FUCHS

Remember the difference you make to those around you.

Too often we underestimate
the power of a touch, a smile,
a kind word, a listening ear,
an honest compliment, or the
smallest act of caring...

this is you!!

LEO BUSCAGLIA

Cultivate kindness.

...it is only with gratitude
that life becomes rich.

DIETRICH BONHOEFFER

Approach each day with thanks.

Enjoy the little things, for
one day you may look back and
realize they were the big things.

ROBERT BRAULT

Make small moments count.

Celebrate the happiness that
friends are always giving...

AMANDA BRADLEY

*Delight in the people who
make life beautiful.*

Those who bring sunshine
to the lives of others cannot
keep it from themselves.

J.M. BARRIE

Share a spark with everyone around you.

Do your little bit of good where you are; it's those little bits of good put together that overwhelm the world.

DESMOND TUTU

Give your gift to the world.

How wonderful it is that
nobody need wait a single
moment before starting to
improve the world.

ANNE FRANK

Make a difference today.

You have been my friend...
That in itself is a tremendous thing.

E.B. WHITE

Be glad for true friends.

I expect to pass through this
world but once. Any good thing,
therefore, that I can do or any
kindness I can show to any human
being, let me do it now. Let me
not defer or neglect it, for I shall
not pass this way again.

STEPHEN GRELLET

Make minor miracles.

you did, you helped
us to keep moving!

Wherever there is a human
being, there is an opportunity
for a kindness.

SENECA

With special thanks to the entire Compendium family.

Text by: M.H. Clark
Design & Illustration by: Jessica Phoenix
Creative Direction by: Sarah Forster
Edits by: Jennifer Pletsch

ISBN 978-1-935414-62-9

2nd printing. Printed in China with soy inks.